Winter in Bangkok

Winter in Bangkok

Gary Dunne

Cheap Red Dress
Sydney, Australia
April 2020

Notes & Acknowledgments:

For over five decades I've kept a writer's journal. Stuffed with notes, clippings, impressions, grand plans and terrible first drafts, these books now fill a shelf.

In 1986, after backpacking around Asia for over a year, I washed up in Bangkok. With cash running out, I took a job teaching English for six months before finally returning home to Sydney.

Over the next two decades, I dipped into my Bangkok journal for inspiration, then self-plagiarism, to produce these fictional snapshots of a unique time in a unique place, now, finally, in print together for the first time.

"Queen Victoria's Statue", *The Adelaide Review,* the late 80s; then *BURN magazine* in the mid-90s.

"Deliverance", *Hard,* BlackWattle Press, 1997.

"Hot Sex in Bangkok", based on a short article for *OutRage* in the late 80s; *Wanderlust,* Thunder's Mouth Press, NY, 2003.

"Five Beach Stories" *Fruit,* BlackWattle Press, 1994.

All four stories were published as an e-book, *The Queen & I,* gay-ebooks, 2006.

CONTENTS

Queen Victoria's Statue

"Hello Simon. I wake you."

"Yes."

"I go to university. I drive you to class."

"Thanks Gow. Ten minutes, OK?"

"No problem. Bye bye." She hangs up.

It's 9am, another seedy Bangkok morning.

Twenty minutes later she arrives and sits politely sipping coffee at my makeshift desk while I pack my briefcase. Even at this hour, I have the feeling she'd prefer Pepsi, 'same same Tina Turner', but I don't have any. Gow's perfectly groomed, no signs of our previous night's drinking. I feel, and probably look, blotchy.

"You have money card." Another question without a rising inflection.

"A credit card?" I ask. She looks serious but it is hard to tell.

"Maybe. Or..." She mimes inserting a card into a terminal and pressing buttons.

"No. I have traveller's cheques. Australian dollars."

"Today you bank baht. Maybe tomorrow coup coming. Maybe bank shutting."

"Oh."

I'm not sure how important or reliable this piece of news is. I go to the wardrobe and collect my passport and cheques from inside the old sandshoe. Judging by the expression on Gow's face, I've picked a perfect hiding place. To Thais, feet are the most unclean part of the body.

"We go now." She glances at my clock. Foreigners are almost expected to be a little uncouth.

"OK."

In the staff room I corner the English queen, a self-proclaimed expert on Thai affairs. He is blasé.

"Of course a coup is possible, my dear. You *do* read the papers?"

"Not for a week or two."

"For the last few days everyone's been denying it. If they keep it up much longer, it'll be on for sure."

"Should we be worried?"

"No. It's rarely a big deal. This country holds the world record for coups. They used to happen all the bloody time. Been a bit quieter since Old Mother Prem took over."

"What about going to the bank?"

"Only get enough for a week or two. Hang on to your real money. It'll be worth more if there's a decent dust-up."

"Is it safe to go out?" I'm half-serious.

"Probably. Just avoid standing between the crowd and the tanks. That sort of thing."

"So, all in all, it's unlikely I'll be shot at."

"Highly unlikely. Unless you happen to be sleeping with the wrong general..."

Page one of the English language morning paper says, NO COUP. Pages two and three have statements from many people with unpronounceable names, claiming, with varying degrees of certainty, that a coup is not being plotted, either by themselves, or by nameless others. It doesn't make much sense. Page five mentions, almost in passing, a small run on the local banks.

I don't function well before noon. For this, and other reasons, my first morning class in 'Advanced Conversational English' is often the most difficult. It's made up of four young computer programmers and one middle management executive. The programmers work and study. Any spare time seems to be devoted to visiting family or going to the temple. Mr Wanchai, the executive, is into bonsai, a topic with even less potential for conversation than either ageing parents or the Buddhist notion of 'making merit'.

With other classes, I only spend half the time on the syllabus topic then we can turn to movies, TV, music, nightclubs and gossip. When caught by the owner of the school, my excuse (half-true) was that my students gain more from these 'unstructured informalities' than from his antique British text books. Most want English for jobs in trade (the males) or to become Thai International hostesses (the females). Either way they'll have to be able to chat.

All attempts at informalities with this morning class however have failed. At the ripe age of thirty-one, Mr Wanchai has only been to a discotheque once. A young man asked him if he was looking for his daughter so he left, vowing never to return. That story was as close as he'd come to saying that he mildly disapproves of my lifestyle, certainly enough to inhibit further frivolous conversations.

We practice buying train tickets from each other then work our way through the vocab necessary to master the intricacies of British Rail. I ad-lib an English update and the American equivalents, doubting if even I am properly equipped for the New York subways.

There's still half an hour to go. I consider moving on to the joys of hailing taxis, but they are tomorrow's lesson, so I mention the headlines instead.
"Yes. Coup is possible."
"Yes. Thailand has many coups."
A complete dead end. The English queen says he deals with unresponsive groups by chalking up, 'my hovercraft is full of eels', but he's never explained how this solves the problem. I'm turning to the pages on taxis when Mr Wanchai suddenly begins speaking.

"My English is not good. In seventies, I am History student. Thammasat University." He points. It's only three blocks away. "The Army are outside the buildings. They attack. Many kill. Many many injury. I am long time downstairs. Basement. We hide. We rip shirts. Bandage. I do bandage on friends. Much blood. We cry because smoke gas. There is fear. Some dear friends die."

He pauses, lights a cigarette, and smiles. "The students love the king. The king love the students. He hears this thing. He say it is a bad thing. The bad general lose much face. He goes to exile is become a monk. There is much democracy and rejoicing. Till next coup coming."

I promise myself I'll get a history book and find out if the official version sounds as mythological. I try telling Mr Wanchai that I can't imagine him, a conservative merchant banker, as a radical student.
"All the radicals and communists in Thailand now finished."
"Why finished?"
"Now have career, carphone and credit facility."
"The same thing is happening in Australia."
"This is American Domino Theory," he says with a smug grin.

The bank is very crowded and they take an unusually long time double-checking and photocopying my passport. Maybe I should stock up on food, but with no fridge, it seems pointless. And anyway, I can't imagine how a city so totally devoted to the production and consumption of snacks can suddenly run out of supplies.

Back home I sleep till 8pm, trying to catch up on hours missed. I wake, bathed in sweat and as tired as ever. Like the stench of exhaust fumes and coriander, the humidity is all pervasive. I ring for ice and head for a shower

Twenty minutes later, I'm sitting on my balcony, drinking iced black coffee laced with a decent slug of Mekhong whisky. It's not much of a view. To the right, rice paddies, for the sun to set behind. To the left, a highway, nearly always packed solid with traffic. It could be anywhere, just a main road through a built-up area, lined with restaurants, car yards, shops, apartment and office buildings. There's no depth to this modernisation. It's all recently completed concrete, glass and metal. Between this and the paddies is an industrial waste zone, part of which serves as a carpark for my apartment block.

The first time he visited, the English queen waxed philosophic from this third floor view-point. "The problem with the Thais is that they take our advice. This city used to be the Venice of the East. Every year the monsoon came. It washed all the shit into the klongs then eventually out to sea. We told them to build highways so they filled them in to make roads. Now the place is slowly sinking in its own mud and shit. Now it floods every monsoon season and the traffic pollution is probably the worst in Asia... The good thing is that generally what they've taken is only a superficial veneer. Underneath, it's still pure Thai."

He went on to talk about city streets collapsing during the last monsoon season and described my view as 'significant'. I called it 'noisy but average' and he told me that the Australian mind is not suited to analytic contemplation.

Maybe he's right. For me, times like this, sitting thinking, are rare. When they do turn up, the best I can achieve is feeling vaguely wistful. The apartment manager once told me that I'm the only foreigner living in this building. It's the kind of statement that looks great in letters home. Actually, it's neither exotic, nor am I alone. I guess that since they've built the Lhasa Hilton, nowhere is exotic anymore. There's a

Pizza Hut Restaurant just down the road, its sign is the brightest of them all. Being alone is equally 'not possible', to use Gow's favourite negative. I'm paid to spend all day communicating, plus there's the exhausting after-hours social life. The real differences are subtler, more disturbing and not so easily glossed over with reassuring neon familiarities.

Towards the end of the second glass of Mekhong ice coffee, I watch the headlights of Gow's Mazda as it pulls into the car park. I throw on shoes, tie and some gel, then hurry down to meet her.

By anyone's standards, she and I make an odd couple. We first met as we were both sneeking out of an unbearably over-polite cocktail party being held to welcome some dickhead from the British Council. I asked her where the nearest main road was so I could hail a tuk-tuk. She offered me a lift. Actually she said something like, "Get in the Mazda. We go somewhere more fun."

At some point during that first night out, perhaps between the second bar and the first night-club, I mentioned I was gay.
"No problem. Same same. I gay too," she replied.
I wasn't sure what that meant. Did she also sleep with men or was she a dyke? I asked if she had women lovers.
"We go to palace later. I show you. Promise. Later."
I must have been fairly drunk. I said something about my Thai manners not being up to an audience with anyone that important.

Eventually I realised that our tour of expensive nightspots was just to kill time before going to The Palace. It was social death to arrive too early. And I doubt if I would have been any less in awe if she had taken me to meet the Thai royal family.

From the outside, The Palace Videotheque is an unassuming concrete monstrosity, halfway between a castle and a factory. Inside, it's huge but ultra-classy. A packed house of nearly five thousand up-market Thais is not uncommon on Saturday nights. At first, I was overwhelmed. It's the size of a dance party but it also has restaurants, bars, fast table service and video arcades. The toilets have hair driers and fresh hot towels. I felt like Damien from Dubbo at his first Mardi Gras party.

Gow has the right contacts. She has her own well-located table where she regularly holds court. Friends come and go. She nibbles popcorn and sips over-garnished cocktails. She rarely dances. It depends on the music, most of which she politely tolerates and that's all.

When we were alone at the table she kept her earlier promise, discreetly pointing out various stunning women, telling me they each had been or currently were her girlfriend. Eventually I stopped believing her and began indicating various men I found attractive, claiming them all as ex-lovers. It was the start of a perfect friendship.

Now, after some months of regular nightclubbing with Gow, I concede that she does in fact know most of these women, but who she actually sleeps with, if anyone, remains a bit of a mystery I've learnt to be too polite to explore.

Tonight we are barely seated when Nik, Nok and Noi, a giggly trio of stylish teenage design students descend upon us. Tonight, they're more excited than usual, there's 'new hi-tech' to experience. It turns out to be a combination of mirror-balls and lasers, the latest innovation to the million dollar video and lighting system above and around the paddock size dance floor. It's lethal, which is maybe why they like it. A direct hit causes temporary blindness. A Thai version of living dangerously.

Back at the table, the volume of the music precludes all but the most basic conversation. Just as well, given that their English and my Thai deteriorate after two cocktails. We play a version of romantic charades which involves discreetly pointing out passers-by who are most likely, or most unlikely, to fancy one or other of us and miming why. The victim then mimes why they are or aren't interested, or equally discreetly points out who this person does fancy and suggests why. It's a game with endless variations given the Thai love of intrigue, innuendo and plain soapie-style gossip.

Lek arrives and flirts quietly. Gow introduced us, her answer to my singular state. (Matchmaking is one of her hobbies. I think she believes people look tidier in pairs.) It's taken me the last month to work out that middle-class Thais flirt much more than we do and sleep around much less. It's all a question of face and I've no intention of losing some by expecting too much, too soon. I flirt back, suggesting a date the next evening, the movies followed by a romantic supper, minus our current entourage. Lek giggles, eyes flashing, then moves on, promising to return, but doesn't. To call it frustrating would be an understatement except that it's happened before and I've virtually given up expecting anything to eventuate.

The English queen says middle class Thais are both the most decadent and the most puritanical people on this planet. I'm beginning to understand what he means. In letters home I talk about Buddhist resignation, not mentioning the cause, feeling like the only celibate foreigner in Bangkok. It's a problem that can be solved quite cheaply, but I'm not about to admit failure and join the ranks of the sweaty sex tourists in Patpong.

After 1am, the crowd shows unexpected signs of thinning. We normally stay till closing, around three, then head on to one of a number of fashionable restaurants for supper. As the sky grows lighter and the first workers and monks of the morning are seen, we head for home, reassured that the economic and spiritual needs of the new day are being attended to.

Tonight however, Gow's jangling car keys at 1-30am.
"We go home now. Nik, Nok and Noi go too."
"No restaurant?"
"Not possible."

The sky is dark and the streets deserted as we speed towards the trio's apartment block. No one speaks. From there, Gow takes several backstreets, ending up on one of her 'short-cuts', a wide unlit road through semi-rural, semi-industrial outer suburbs. The speedo hits 140 kph and I realise that we are both more drunk than usual. We normally sober up over supper and coffees.
"You never use a seatbelt," I comment, doing mine up.
"Not important. I am good driver."
"In Australia, seatbelt is law. Must do." Sounding pompous.
"Not necessary," she says and accelerates.

Times like this I'm out of my depth. I don't know if it's her fatalism, a Buddhist belief in que sera sera, or just chic recklessness. Maybe it all amounts to the same thing.

In the distance there's a line of very bright lights across the otherwise empty road. It takes us ages to slow down to a crawl and stop at the roadblock. I've never seen one before, not in Thailand anyway. There's several large grey tanks and a number of well-armed soldiers in tight uniforms. One approaches, shining his torch straight at the windscreen. I can't see his face. Others casually hold semi-automatic rifles and watch. I fumble through my pockets as Gow hands over her ID card and some papers. He takes his time reading them.

Ignoring my offered passport, he returns her belongings and waves us through the check-point. We take off at great speed.
"No problem," she says, laughing. "My father very

important man."
"What does he do?"
"Make much money."
I laugh, then realise she's serious.

I oversleep and am late for work. It's a sickly morning. Mr Wanchai is unimpressed and the lesson on hailing taxis is painfully slow. Just before lunch, Lek rings.
"Tonight we go movies."
"Sure. Yes." I'm surprised.
"Siam Centre steps. Seven o'clock. Possible?"
"No problem."
"OK. Bye bye."

In the staff room, the English queen is lecturing on his usual theme, the unfathomability of the Oriental mind.
"Take Queen Victoria's statue for example. The old girl used to be outside our embassy. Then the word spread that the Empress had no problem with issue. Gave birth every spring. Next thing you know the infertile of Bangkok are queuing up with flowers and presents. Queen Vic, the Earth Mother..."
"Not amused."
"Hardly. They've moved her inside the gates, but there's still always fresh flowers around the base."

Then, for the benefit of 'those who slept in', he re-explains the morning papers. There's a photo of someone important paying homage to someone more important.
"It means no-one loses face and the political crisis is over."
"Obvious really."

We foreigners all laugh. It's as obvious as anything else in this sinking city of gold, glass and chrome. For as outsiders, all we can see is what's reflected from those gleaming surfaces.

Deliverance

Gow has solved my inability to get to work on time. She's found me a motor cycle boy. He's about nineteen and he rides a sleek, powerful Suzuki. Each weekday morning at around 8:30, he pulls up in the car-park next to my building and lights a cigarette. If I haven't come out or at least waved from my balcony by the time he flicks the butt away, he comes up, bangs on my door until I respond, then goes back downstairs to wait. He charges ten baht extra for the wake-up service.

Before I met him, my mornings were chaotic. I live some six kilometres from the language school. Even if I don't sleep in, the buses are unreliable. It's not that they don't turn up, the problem is that three days out of five, Bangkok traffic comes to a complete stand still. There's nothing to be done but sit and wait, which the Thais, being Thais, do with far more grace than anyone else, especially me.

Sometimes I'd get off the bus and walk. Either way, the result was the same. I'd rush in late for my first class looking like a bloated, sweating pig. My students would always be sitting there, elegant and relaxed, poised to start work. They're far too polite to complain which only made it worse.

Those days are over. Each morning I now climb behind then

wrap my body around my motor cycle boy. He goes very fast, our speed being due to the fact that he rarely takes up one whole lane. We ride between the lines of cars and buses. Even when the traffic is completely grid-locked, we fly. He's skilled. We cruise through impossible gaps with barely centimetres on either side. Should he misjudge, the first points of contact would be my knees which is why our bodies are so tightly joined, and why I'm developing thigh definition.

If this was Bali, he'd be a Kuta cowboy. It's a total look. He wears boots, tight jeans, and a sleeveless top. With dragons tattooed around both upper arms, hair gelled back, aviator shades and cigarette, my motor cycle boy astride his gleaming Suzuki is hot property and he totally knows it. I've been hooked since day one and I'm sure he knows that too. He speaks no English and doesn't follow my Thai. It's impossible to guess what's behind his quietly arrogant attitude to everything, including me.

On the first day, he insisted I grip his hips rather than the back of the seat behind me. I was very tense. I knew his bike was both his passion and his sole source of income. There wasn't a single scratch on it. I had to be reasonably safe. Despite his attitude, he knew his limitations. The risks were calculated. My body however would freeze with fear, knowing how fast we were going and how close we were to the cars on either side of us. I'd never felt so vulnerable.

Then my body began to trust him. I'd relax, sense his intentions and respond. We began to go much faster. Our ability to weave with pinpoint accuracy through the clogged arteries of Bangkok is based on us being a single unit with him in total control. That physical trust and communication developed gradually. I now know when he's going to accelerate, brake or lean, and we now share something close to exhilaration when he hits top gear.

Today, he's about half an hour early, banging on my door at 8am. I insist he come in and have coffee while I get my act together. I point to the clock radio. He shrugs his shoulders and starts looking through my tape collection.

I leave the front door open. Gow explained ages ago that if you have a single visitor and you shut the front door, it means you are having sex. There are many idiosyncrasies to Thai apartment living and most of Gow's explanations of them make even less sense. I'm aware that by middle-class standards my apartment is mildly embarrassing. It's a concrete box with a thin balcony, a built-in wardrobe and a primitive en-suite bathroom. There's a mattress on the floor, a phone and, near the balcony, a laminex topped table and two old vinyl chairs. These came with the lease. All I've added are a jug, a fan, a clock radio and domestic nick-nacks. It's a balance between my desire to be comfortable and the knowledge that it will all be left behind when I leave.

I make coffee and pour two cups. He takes a seat. I find him an ashtray then head for a quick shower and shave. When I come out I notice that he's shut the front door and turned his chair around to face the room. I am naked. He is observing me. The air is electric.

I know his body so intimately, from the smell of his hair and skin to the way his washboard stomach ripples as we weave through the traffic. He's felt my initial terror and fear of being knee-capped. He's felt it evolve into absolute faith. On the bike, I respond and flow with his every movement. Here, in my room, he's still in total control and he knows it.

We watch each other intently. I slowly dry myself. He sprawls back in his chair, opening his legs. I throw my towel onto the bed. He unbuttons his vest. His physical presence is overwhelming. He yawns and stretches, exposing more of his flawless torso. I stare in adoration. He knows what I want.

He smiles and lights a cigarette, fully aware that the next move is his. He watches as I drink my coffee then put on aftershave. I roll deodorant in my arm pits. I gel and comb my hair in the mirror. I run out of things to do. He casually puffs smoke at me. I turn and stand naked before him, semi-aroused. He brushes the bulge in the front of his jeans as if removing biscuit crumbs. I look him straight in the eye. He takes another long drag on his cigarette and blows more smoke. I am shameless. I glance to his groin, to the bed, and back to his eyes again.

But he doesn't respond. Then he laughs, sits up straight, stubs out his cigarette and gestures at the clock radio. 8:24. I shrug my shoulders and say in Thai that it doesn't matter. He stands up and gestures uncompromisingly at the open wardrobe. I obey and we leave on time.

This morning we fly faster than ever through the narrow corridors between the cars. My body is aware of nothing beyond being an extension of his. We weave, brake and accelerate sharply. We do small wheel stands at every set of lights. My fingers caress from his hips to his ribs and back. I breathe through his hair, oblivious to everything but our easy synchronisation.

At school, I climb off and breathlessly thank him using the polite form appropriate for those one respects. The motor cycle boy laughs. He offers me a cigarette, then lights it. I get out my wallet. He takes it from me, removes forty baht, the standard fare, no wake-up surcharge, then hands my wallet back. He thanks me using exactly the same polite words.

Hot Sex in Bangkok

One of the highlights of being a resident of Bangkok is observing the tabloid tourists doing Patpong, the red-light area. These mixed packs of large, colourfully dressed westerners can always be seen late at night cruising around in search of something really awful. They usually end up in one of those laminex bars where Thai women, each with a plastic number pinned to her scanty costume, dance on small stages. By the time the ice has melted in their one, grossly overpriced drink, they've seen some man pay the bar for the right to take one of the women upstairs or home for the night. Everyone is in agreement that it's absolutely terrible, degrading, and someone, maybe *Sixty Minutes*, ought to do something about it. And they leave, armed with a great story to liven up a dinner party when they get back to the real world.

Whenever I mix with foreigners, I keep hearing the same story again and again. The sex bars are shockingly lurid and not to be missed. The English queen can't believe that I've never been inside one.

"It's the moral outrage," I explain. "I'm no good at moral outrage."

"Look at it this way," he replies. "Do you really want to leave Bangkok without having seen at least one live sex show full of tacky sleaze?"

"It's not my style. I don't care how far a girl can fire a ping-pong ball from her cunt."

"They do have *boy* bars. I know just the place, The Shark Tank. If you're interested, we can go there tonight."

He can be very persistent but, this time, it isn't necessary.

"OK. Let's do it."

I don't apologise. Being totally honest, I guess there's a touch of the tabloid in even the nicest of us.

Once our evening classes have finished we retire to the nearby open-air bar. After a bottle or so of Mekhong, he decides it's late enough and we catch a taxi to Suriwong Road. From there it's a short stroll down a laneway and up a flight of stairs to a cosy, ultra-airconned bar.

We seem to be the only foreigners in the place. Then I notice two Japanese businessmen near the back wall. They are being quietly chatted up by three G-strung boys, each with a plastic number tag (13, 24 and 32) pinned prominently to his open dressing gown. A number of older Thai men sit nearby in armchairs, intent on conversation with each other. The front tables and bar stools are occupied by late-teen Thai yuppies, mainly straight couples, all knocking back over-garnished cocktails and ignoring the American gay porn on video screens on the walls.

My guide orders G&T's. To our left, at the end of the bar, is a small stage on which three boys in see-thru briefs are dancing. It's strange dancing, maximum effect for minimum movement. Their feet seem glued to the stage. Every five minutes or so another trio replaces them, each boy's plastic number either in hand or pinned to his thin costume.

"My dear, it improves after midnight," I am advised. "Just watch out for the manager, she's pushy."

He is. He hovers at my elbow, a large Chinese-Thai person of indeterminate gender with a round face, permanent smile and two prominent gold teeth. His sales pitch is slick and unavoidable. I make a fatal opening mistake by admitting this is my first time. He launches into an explanation of the bar fee system. It's as the tabloid tourists foretold. You pay the bar 150 baht so that you and your intended can leave. Later you "make private arrangements" which include "a gift". The amount is "up to you". When pushed he suggests, "maybe 300 baht".

"My boys," he assures me, "are best in Bangkok. All young, hot sex. All good boys, show much respect, hundred per cent honest. All have test, hundred per cent very clean."
I suggest that I'll have a drink or two and think about choices later.

The hard-sell, however, isn't over. The manager brings out a thick photo album and insists I view every page. It's filled with glossy colour nude shots. Each boy is splayed centre-stage in exactly the same unimaginative pose, clearly showing off his teeth, his erection and his plastic number tag. None look very happy.

My guide has slipped away to an armchair near the back wall and keeps toasting me and winking as the manager continues. I'm being asked about my personal sexual predilections. My reply is vague. I don't want him fixing me up with a date. He explains that all tastes are catered for here from "kings and queens" to "all-'merican kinky sex fun". Anything is possible. Nothing is too much trouble.

I apologise, ask directions to the toilet and make my escape.

While crossing the bar, I realise that I'm probably a bit drunk. We should have had a meal before coming here. I also realise that I'm disappointed. I was expecting a voyeuristic thrill or two with maybe some intimate audience participation, lap dancing, or its Thai equivalent. Not that I was planning on doing anything really sexual, I'm not the type who pays for it, but hot sleaze was what I envisioned, not this cold, clean, neon-lit bar with the carnal ambience of a Pizza Hut, and a manager who should be selling Amway.

Of late, erotic disappointment has loomed large in my life. I now have a Thai boy-friend, Lek. We go to the movies as a couple. We go to dinner as a couple. We go nightclubbing with friends as a couple. We do everything most couples do, except fuck. I'm sure we will, eventually. It's all a matter of time. It took him a month to agree to going to the movies. A week later we were kissing good night at my front door. Another week later we kissed horizontally while on a picnic in the park. It was obvious that we were both aroused, but unzipping was still out of the question. One weekend, as soon as we're both free, we're going away, overnight, to Ayuthaya, the old capital, about 100 kms north, and, as always, I have great expectations. Which is a long-winded way of saying I'm sexually frustrated.

The Men's is spectacularly tacky. There are spotlights above every plastic gilt-edged mirror and gaudy fixture. The attendant, a svelte queen with over-permed hair, jumps to his feet and greets me with a big friendly smile and polite bow. It occurs to me that he and the manager are the only staff in the whole place who are wearing trousers.

I register the hot towel oven, blow driers, jars of gel and body lotions, cans of hairspray, and a whole shelf of familiar designer-label colognes and aftershaves. His vanity units each have two taps. I beam a grin right back at him. I haven't experienced hot running water in months. I intend to indulge myself. I may go home sexually disappointed (what's new) but at least I'll feel and smell totally fabulous.

The attendant massages my shoulders and neck while I pee. I moan encouragingly and he works harder. I undo my shirt and almost bathe in the basin. He lets me use extra hot towels and go to town on all the beauty products. My enthusiasm is infectious. He wants to blow-dry, spray and style my hair, but I know a zooshy-do practitioner when I meet one, so I don't let him. He seems genuinely disappointed. I leave a generous tip and exit, red-faced and reeking of fake Eternity. (Tourist Tip #29: Sniff any designer-label scents before liberally applying.)

The manager, thankfully, is nowhere in sight. There's a cute young Thai in pure white Y-fronts perched on the arm of the English queen's chair. I saunter over and take the armchair next to them. His tag says 47, his briefs say Calvin Klein, and, his name, he says, is Nik. Up close, he's even better looking.

Nik thinks her majesty is a "very sexy man" who will, he suggests, buy the three of us a drink. I say no, it's my shout, and Nik signals to the barman. Any remnants of a grumpy mood evaporate as I watch my friend ever-so-politely resist the wandering hands and erotic hard-sell. I love observing Brits under fire, their manners are always so impeccable. And Nik's brilliant at his trade, constantly flattering, prick-tempting and teasing, a right little heart-breaker. The drinks cost a fortune and I don't mind at all.

On stage a new performance is beginning. Nik explains that it's called The Big Cock And Masturbation Show. The same trios of young men, now naked and wanking, are still dancing without moving their feet. It's pretty unerotic, given their blank expressions and the audience's complete lack of interest. The yuppies' tables are littered with cocktail debris, paper umbrellas and lemon twists; the air thick from their imported Marlboros, puffed not smoked. The Japanese leave discretely, taking numbers 13 and 32 with them. Their places are taken by a pair of Thai suits who look like they too are only after a quick take-away before supper.

Nik finally establishes that the queen and I are an item. He suggests a "sexy threeway", which my friend firmly rejects. Nik politely thanks me for the drink, bids us both a friendly farewell and moves on to try his luck with the Thai businessmen.

"He'll tell the others we're a couple and we should be left alone."

"You don't fancy him?" I ask with suitable fake incredulity.

"Of course I fancy him but I've got an equally hot Thai boyfriend waiting in bed at home. Do you fancy him?"

"Maybe," I reply cautiously, "But I've got a boyfriend too."

"Your yuppie disco accessory?"

"His name is Lek."

"So she's now your boyfriend. Congratulations. Obviously I was quite wrong about her."

"Indeed."

"And you're totally satisfied? You don't fancy a quick fuck on the side, no strings attached."

"Correct."

"It's simply that as your guide, it's my job to see that you're aware of all the possibilities."

"I'm fine thanks."

While he's ordering another round of drinks, I watch one of the Thai businessman pay the bar fee and leave with Nik.

I sulk in silence through The Big Suck And Fuck Show, a bland combination of gymnastics and gay sex. Each position is repeated at various locations on the stage so everyone can see what's going where. No one, including the performers, seems that interested.

We are being hassled to buy drinks by numbers 7, 9 and 24. They begin classic Suzi Wong conversations. 'What your name?' 'You sexy man. How long you stay Bangkok?' 'What country you come?' 'I know Australia. Have good

Sydney friend, Mr Daryl. You know him?'

They don't have Nik's disarming looks or charm. I answer in equally fractured Thai which maybe lowers their enthusiasm and expectations. It's surprising sometimes how much conversation can be drawn out of a working vocab of twenty words in another language. Obviously enough for a one night stand.

Number 24 is babbling, an incomprehensible mix of English and Thai, about the highlight of the next show which is about to begin. I whisper to my friend that perhaps it's time to go. I've seen enough for one night.
"Quite right, my dear. Perfect timing. I always leave before they bring on the Alsatian."

Bangkok's humidity seems worst whenever you exit anywhere airconditioned. Stepping out onto the footpath is like entering a sauna filled with compost and exhaust fumes. We adjourn to the nearest greasy wok for supper.

"Well, at least I can say I've seen it," I announce flatly.
"And how's your moral outrage?" he asks, pouring me a glass of Mekhong.
"It wasn't what I was expecting. The hard-sell makes it kind of unreal. It's too easy, too sterile. We're buying, we've got money. They're selling, they need money. I can't imagine myself actually bunging 150 baht on the bar and ordering a number 69 to go, hold the anchovies. I think I was expecting something less business-like. It certainly wasn't erotic."

"Raw capitalism rarely is."

"I'm glad I'm a socialist."

"You Australians and your socialism. Everyone has to be equal. You always have to split every bill. Thais don't think like that. The richest person picks up the tab. We're 'ferung', foreign, ergo we're rich, ergo we pay. Your real problem is pride. You simply don't like the idea of having to pay for sex. What do you think your affair with Lek is based on? Who pays the big bills when you two go out to those expensive nightclubs?"

I'm tempted to try justifying things like love and commitment, but I suspect he'd demolish a romantic argument in seconds flat. Plus I'm not so sure I really believe in it myself.

"My relationship with Lek is based on more than just money." I reply. "I merely happen to earn a lot more of it than he does."

"Exactly. Which is why I keep telling you, you can do better than an upwardly mobile prick-teaser. For a similar weekly investment, in cash rather than cocktails and restaurants, you could have a hot young Thai living with you. All the rich queens have one, expats and locals alike. Even Old Mother Prem has that hunky chauffeur he takes everywhere with him. Think about it. Your own well-mannered, well-hung house-boy. No middle-class scruples, no expensive tastes. With luck he might even cook or clean. Mine, unfortunately, refuses. That's why we hire staff when we entertain."

"You've seen my place. It's not a huge apartment like you two have. It's a hovel, barely suitable for one," I reply. "I don't need, or want, a paid house boy."

"If that's too morally offensive, for the cost of a round of cocktails you can pick up a boy for the night. Lek will never know, not that he's being faithful to you anyway. You only see him once or twice a week. You can bet he's out and about on the other nights.

"And before you start talking about exploitation, try looking closer to home. Ask yourself if someone like Nik would trade places with that young kid who cleans our classrooms and toilets every evening for probably around 200 baht a week. I don't think so. Not when he can make that much in an hour.

"And you aren't going to try and tell me you didn't find young Nik the slightest bit attractive. When he and that banker left, your tongue was hanging out with jealousy. I know. I could see it, even from way over at the bar. And believe me, it wasn't a pleasant sight. Mind you, he was a cut above the usual trash we ferungs attract around here. Even I was sorely tempted. Nik could make a happy man feel very old."

"You win," I admit, mainly because he has. "Like I said, I'm no good at moral outrage. I'm too easily corrupted. Maybe next time. I did like the bathroom up there. You should have checked it out. Unbelievable. It would be worth a return visit just for another round with their beauty products."

"Next time go easy on their fake colognes. If anyone stinks like a whore around here, it's ..." He pauses mid-sentence and starts waving furiously at a passing Thai student, "Speak of the devil."

It takes me several seconds to realise that it's Nik, casually dressed and carrying a small backpack, presumably returning to the bar up the laneway. He comes over and greets us both by name.

"Do you have time for another drink," says the English queen, offering him the stool next to me and the bottle of Mekhong.

"No problem," says Nik, and, in Thai, asks the proprietor for a Pepsi, then sits down.

"You not find boyfriends in the bar?" he asks.

"We had to leave, it was too cold," I reply.

"My friend Tui says ferung countries all very cold. Ferungs like very cold."

"Not all ferungs," says my friend. "Some like it hot... That's why we live in Bangkok."

"How long you live in Bangkok?"

"I've been here too long," he replies. "Simon, maybe a few months. I told a big lie back in the bar. We work together, teaching English, but we aren't a couple. I've been living with my Thai partner for over a year. But my colonial friend here is very single. And available. She's really not my type. Two queens together, no good. It would never work. Too much gossip, no sex."

Nik laughs.

"Are you from Bangkok?" I ask.

Nik is Isaan, from Udorn Thani up near the Lao border. He learnt English hanging around the local US military base as a child. He's in Bangkok to complete a uni degree in economics and commerce, and also attends an advanced language class early evenings. It's a school we haven't heard of, which makes sense when he explains that he's studying Japanese.

Throughout this conversation I'm aware that Nik's knee is

rubbing against mine under the table. He's quietly flirting with me. At last, familiar gay territory. I flirt back. The eye contact is immediately reciprocated.

I tell him about the joys of teaching English, the casual conversation videos we are about to star in, and I list my favourite nightclubs.

"I love The Palace. I dance same same Michael Jackson," says Nik. "But Palace very expensive for poor student. Maybe you take me there?"

"Good heavens, is that the time?" says the English queen, glancing at his watch and faking a huge yawn. "I must be on my way. The boyfriend turns frigid if I stay out after midnight."

He shakes Nik's hand, "It's been a real pleasure meeting you Nik. Good luck with the Japanese." And he adds a paragraph in rapid-fire Thai that I don't catch.

Nik smiles and responds, promising something, but again my Thai isn't good enough to understand.

"And you my dear, vous comprendez la franglaiz?" he asks while shaking my hand. I nod and he continues in a fast flat monotone, "Donnez votre chaud trade, um, trios centenaries, not avant, mais après la grande bonk. OK?"

"Mercy, madam," I reply and nod again.

We watch a contented man head off down the street.

Nik finishes his Pepsi, smiles and takes my hand, "We go your apartment now."

I pay the bill and we leave.

I'm almost nervous as I open my front door. It's been two or three years since I brought trade home. I've been travelling, and before that, in Australia, I spent a year or so being too neurotic about Aids to successfully score anything but Serepax. There has been the odd, occasional fuck while on the road, but it's always something serendipitous, never a full-on pick up like this.

Nik shuts the door and starts kissing me.
"You go washroom at bar?" he asks. "Sexy aftershave."
I laugh, "Too much sexy aftershave. But it's great. I had fun there."
"Tui my good friend. He always fun. He makes my haircut. Much style. He teach me washroom massage."
Nik begins massaging my shoulders and neck. I moan theatrically and he starts tickling me under the arms.

Soon we are rolling on the mattress, undressing each other. I'm surprised to discover big candy-striped boxers beneath his loose cotton slacks.
"Where are your Calvins?" I ask.
He looks confused.
"Your white underpants?" I explain.
"Very sexy briefs," he replies. "Very small. I only have in bar. I like boxer shorts."
"They're very sexy too," I say, unconvincingly.
"We go washroom now," he replies and pulls them off. He already has an erection.

My bathroom is very primitive, nothing like the facilities at the bar. There's a squat toilet, a drain, and two cold water taps; one low, one high. I've connected a shower head to the top tap and it's functional. Water goes everywhere but eventually ends up running down the drain or toilet.

We wash each other. His body is almost hairless, a rich dusty brown, quite dark for a Thai, and he's slim and lithe, built like a dancer. Up close I realise that his small rectangular patch of pubic hair is too small and too rectangular.

"You shave?" I ask, looking up.

"Tui makes haircut," he explains. "Tui makes all boys haircut at bar. He says ferungs like boys very young, no cock hair. Good for business."

"How old are you?" I ask. Going by his verbal CV, I guess early, maybe mid-twenties. Going by his body, he could be anything from late teens upwards. It's really hard to guess a Thai person's age.

"Sixteen."

One good lie deserves another. "I'm twenty two," I say.

Back on the bed we kiss and romp. Nik's playful, exploring what turns me on and what doesn't. He's harder to read, mainly because he's had a bone-hard erection ever since he kicked off those daggy extra-large boxers. He's a passionate kisser and his other oral skills are as finely honed.

"We fuck now," he finally says and rolls over, then unzips his backpack.

"Not necessary," I suggest and get up. "I have plenty of condoms."

I hand him the Australia Post box I received from home a month or so ago. The Smarties, Scotch Finger biscuits, Vegemite and other goodies, all since consumed, were buried within this huge assortment of sachets of lube, and condoms: plain, ribbed and coloured.

"You always do safe sex?" I ask, wondering if now's the time for a lecture.

"No problem," says Nik. He rips open an orange condom, unrolls it, blows it up to balloon size and lets it go. It jets out over the low balcony wall and into the night. He pushes me onto my back, kneels between my knees, opens a black condom and giggles as he rolls it on himself.

"Big black cock. Same same Michael Jackson."

"I think his is smaller," I reply.

I lift my legs and apply some KY. He takes his time. We maintain total eye contact as he fully penetrates me. Then we begin slow fucking. We kiss deeply. I notice that his eyes are still open and for some unclear reason this means a lot to me.

It's as if we've been lovers for years. We pulse together with an intensity that keeps on building. Just when I think he's about to come, he stops, changes our position, and the intensity starts all over again. He won't let me touch myself, concerned, accurately I guess, that any direct stimulation and I'll come in seconds flat. He keeps me in this quivering state seemingly forever.

Finally I'm on my back yet again, my knees as earrings, and he's really pumping. Without loosing momentum he slips one hand between us and begins wanking me. His timing is perfect. We orgasm in unison.

Bliss.

Eventually he withdraws, throws the condom at the bedside bin and lies down next to me. His body has an erotic sweaty sheen. I'm dripping like a collapsed marathon runner.
"You number one, Simon. Very sexy man," he whispers in my ear.
"Phew... Nik," I reply breathlessly, "Phew... That was... incredible. Thank you."
"Your friend say you need long time, hard fuck." He nods at the bedside alarm clock. It's 1:52. "We fuck thirty two minutes," he says proudly. "You like?"
All I can do is nod.

Nik kisses my cheek, reaches over and grabs a towel. After wiping us both off, he gathers the other towel and his backpack.
"I go washroom now," he says.

I heave a long sigh, get up and consider changing the bed linen which is dark with sweat, all of it mine. Nik's good. The best sex I've had in years. I pick the black condom up from the floor and drop it into the bin. It isn't loaded. Nik's better than good. I check my wallet then raid the emergency cash supply in the wardrobe for 100 baht notes.

He spends ages in the bathroom. I wrap on a sarong, make a pot of tea and sit on the balcony smoking the best cigarette I've tasted in years, listening to the sound of him brushing his teeth and gargling.

Nik finally emerges and dresses quickly. He doesn't want tea. He styles his hair in my small mirror before returning his brush, comb and gel to his pack.
"I go home now," he says and kisses me on the cheek.
"Any chance I can see you again?" I ask.
"I'm always at the bar Friday Saturday nights. Maybe other night. Always Friday and Saturday."

He pulls his wallet from his back pocket and extracts a business card which he hands to me. On one side it has a simple map showing how to get to The Shark Tank from Suriwong Road. On the other, the bar's logo, address, phone number and hours are printed in English and Thai, along with the name NIK clearly hand-written below a quick sketch of a number 47 bar tag. It looks like a rough coat of arms.

This is not exactly what I was expecting. I hand him the money, four one hundred baht notes, and, remembering the manager's euphemism, say, "For you Nik. A gift."

Nik formally thanks me in Thai, bowing, his hands together as if praying, the full traditional wai. He then drops to his knees and touches his forehead on my bare feet.

I'm mortified.

He stands up, kisses my cheek yet again, and opens the

front door.

"Friday," he says, "Come to bar Friday, early, before nine o'clock. You talk manager. Order number forty seven. No talk to other boys. I come. We go dinner and nightclub. The Palace. We dance same same Michael Jackson. We make long time sexy love all night."

A final kiss and he's gone.

I sit on the balcony, sipping tea and wistfully calculating the potential cost of such a night of long time sexy love: the bar fee, his 'gift', one classy meal, two Palace tickets, three or four taxis, maybe supper afterwards, and certainly drinks at every venue. It comes to well over US$100, more than half a week's wages, or a month's rent for this concrete box.

But economics can't touch my mood. I've been thoroughly laid and I'm euphoric. The scent of fake Eternity lingers. I smell and feel totally fabulous.

Five Beach Stories

We finally get here. The pair of us are sitting on a verandah watching the waves plop on the nearby shore. We could be anywhere. In fact, we are on some island in the Gulf of Siam. It's hot and there are palm trees. There's also crystal clear ocean and the sand is whiter than the skins of the kids lying around on it. It's tranquil and friendly – low budget tourism at its best. If that's what you want, it's perfect.

I now doubt if it is what we want. The English queen is at his Noel Coward worst, politely pompous and over-organised. I'm short tempered and snappy. We know why we are grumpy and blame it on body chemistry. We're not enjoying withdrawing from nearly six months non-stop work and social-life in Bangkok. Neither of us is ready to sit back and do nothing.

This whole set-up – the beach, the huts and the restaurants – is tailor-made for the hundreds of American college students who are here on vacation. They're everywhere. They insist on sitting with us in the adjoining restaurant and on the beach. Along the way someone has encouraged them to talk about themselves as loudly and as often as they can.

Within two hours we've learnt more than enough about

contemporary American youth. They all have strange names like Rip, Trent, Kari and Griffin. They are far too clean-cut and earnest. If it weren't for their liking of hash cookies they could have all stepped straight out of a sixties B-grade movie.

The first night we hear Beach Stories #1 and #2, each about six times.
"I was on this motor bike. I like fell off. I was in cutoffs and a tee. Now I'm covered in these pus-filled sores. It's gross."
and
"The first day here I got totally lobstered. Now I'm like, peeling."
The new ugly Americans.

We try another restaurant for breakfast and meet a mob of Australians. The Australians are similar to the Americans except that they wear less on the beach and they are more willing to interact with the local environment; plus there are more of them. We hear several versions of Beach Stories #3 and #4.
"I met this Thai girl. We roolly love each other even though we don't understand each other's lingo. It's just the best. After a week here, we're going up north. I'm meeting her family."
and
"We had these biscuits with dope in them. I saw God, maybe it was Buddha, anyway, I ate this huge lunch, spewed my guts up, then couldn't move for hours. Bombed on the beach for the rest of the day. Got burnt real bad but... You had to be there."

That night we're invited to a party at a restaurant further up the beach. Some of the Brady Bunch have taken drugs and are wandering around exploring their own and each other's post-adolescent traumas. The rest have drunk too much and are falling over a lot. There's a mediocre sound system and no special lighting.

We can't help but compare it to Bangkok, the nightclubbing capital of Asia, and wonder why they've bothered to come all the way down here if all they want to do is party. Perhaps because here, unlike Bangkok, unless they've collared one, they don't have to deal with that many Thais. And maybe that's what they want, an easy social setting where the language barrier doesn't exist. There are no unfamiliar nuances in my chat up conversation with a cute Dutch boy sitting alone at the next table. He arrived today and is staying in a hut near ours. And he's very stoned so he's going home now to sleep it off.

The English queen is bored and suggests we move on. Further along the beach we find a restaurant containing a self-contained clique of heavy-duty dope smokers. None of them seems to have much to say to anyone. Some of them don't seem capable of speech. It turns out to be the only restaurant for miles that doesn't show pirated videos of American movies. The surrounding silence is perfect.

We drink and watch the fishing boats far out at sea, at first assuming they are lights on the distant coast of Vietnam. The moon's nearly full. The water's phosphorescent, there are fires on the beach and the palms are silhouetted against the dark blue sky. A drink or two later we find we like each other again.

I wake with a hangover. All the bitter and twisteds have gone as we set out to explore the neighbourhood. The English queen finds a decent second-hand bookshop and I find a little place that sells home-made G-strings. He says I'll look funny with a white Tasmania instead of a Speedo line under my belly button, but I know better.

Over the next few days we settle into an easy routine; breakfast at the restaurant near our hut, swimming, a liquid lunch at one of the many beach-front bars, an afternoon nap then dinner at the quiet restaurant. My bum burns and he finishes a couple of Thomas Hardy novels. We consume much Mekhong. We talk a lot about life and the need for sensible shoes. There's time to do all that and more.

One lunch-time our serenity is disrupted. Sashaying towards the bar is a slim young Thai in short, tight cutoffs, her shirt knotted somewhere between navel and nipples. A local version of Carmen Miranda, minus the fruity hat, she's the 'lady-boy' we've heard much about, a visiting relative of a nearby restaurant owner.

"My name is Diana, what's yours," she announces.

"This is Dame Edna from Australia. She's going to buy us all a drink."

"Hello Damenna."

"And this is Princess Margaret from England. She drinks too much."

Diana helps herself to my cigarettes and makes herself comfortable. I order another bottle of Mekhong. Within minutes a lot of information is exchanged. Diana is taking a break from a hectic career as a performer in Bangkok. Once she discovers that we know our nightclubs, she is reticent about saying exactly where.

"Not a sex show. I am artiste. Katoi. I do numbers in cabaret show. Diana Ross. You know Diana Ross."

"Not personally."

"Now on holiday. Look for new husband. Rich ferung husband. Maybe Merican."

"Not much chance of a husband here. We've checked out the whole island. Many men. No husbands."

"The story of his life," adds the English queen.

"You not try hard," says Diana. "Everywhere plenty husbands. We have big party tonight. Our restaurant. You come. We all get husbands. I do show."

"OK. We'll be there."

"Bring many friends. Big party."

She takes another cigarette before moving on to cold sell the event to the college kids on the other side of the bar.

The party shows no signs of being any different to previous ones we've attended. Diana is nowhere to be found. By midnight people are falling over or deeply examining navels. Suddenly the music stops, the lights go out then a small floodlight shines next to the sound system. Diana Ross hits the stage in a long clinging black dress and the most impressive wig and eye-lashes combination I've seen in years.

She performs 'Chain reaction'. The crowd love it. A severe dose of exotic glamour in a sea of cutoff jeans. And both of us, who've seen enough drag shows to know talent when we see it, are impressed. The body may be Thai but the gestures, the eyes and mouth are pure Miss Ross. To thunderous applause she works her way through a medley of Diana's recent hits before encores of 'Chain reaction' and 'Ain't no mountain high enough'.

Ten minutes later she's at our table. We offer praise, a drink and a cigarette. She accepts all three with ease. The party is going well. She joins the English queen and I in an impromptu, a cappella version of 'Stop in the name of love', all three of us surprised at how in synch our hand gestures are. We offer to join Diana in a show, a revival of the Supremes that will have Bangkok on its knees.

Diana politely smiles, unsure if we are serious. "You watch video and make practice. Many days. With mirror and video. Freeze-frame, copy, freeze-frame, copy. Practice. You need to shave tits, get frocks, much practice. Maybe. Maybe."
"She means, don't give up your day job," I suggest.

Diana motors left, working the crowd. We wonder if it's time to go. Then we spot her heading up the beach, arm in arm with our neighbour, the young Dutch back-packer I've fancied since that first party and the following morning when he appeared on the beach in faded blue Speedos.
"At least someone has found a husband."
"Jealous?" he asks.

"Yes," I reply.
"Another bottle?"
"Why not."

Half an hour later, Diana returns, dancing up the beach and through the restaurant to our table, shoes in hand, dress and wig askew.

"No good husband. Quickie boyfriend. I say, no money, no honey. Maybe Pattaya better. Older mans have plenty money. Here only quickie boyfriend."

She helps herself to a cigarette and my glass of Mekhong, but is too wild-eyed and restless to sit down.

"You're quite right. Quickies are no good. Like Diana Ross says, you can't hurry love," suggests the English queen.

"No good," Diana replies. "And my shoe. Broken." She opens her clutch bag and shows us a long stiletto heel. "Must go. Plenty husbands here. Bye bye."

We finish the bottle watching Diana rapidly circulate around the bar pausing only to briefly cruise any male who catches her eye.

"For someone disappointed in love, she's recovered quickly," I comment.

"She's off her dial," says the English queen. "Blue Speedos might have had no money, but I reckon he must have a stash of something good."

Back at the hut we're both a bit depressed. We talk about why it is that three gay men from totally different parts of the globe are capable of perfect gesture and lip-synch to Diana Ross. We come up with a theory of tribal style based on camp osmosis from an early age. We talk about our favourite nightclubs and bars at home. I talk about those who've died; my friends, Tom and Dave. Then there's the longer list, friends who've tested positive: Pointy Head, Matt, Luke, and, most recently and unexpectedly, my ex, Christian.

He has similar lists and stories. I ask if they explain packing his bags and heading for the Orient a couple of years ago. A similar tale to mine. An urgent need to leave all that behind and go somewhere new.
"I think I would have left anyway. It was simply time to move on."
"Aren't you going to head back some day?" I ask.
"Back to what?"
"England. I mean, I've been here, it seems for ages, but I'm not planning on permanent exile. I'll leave eventually."
"Right now, I'm in no rush to go anywhere."

I suddenly realise that, unlike him, I am, for the first time in ages, feeling quite homesick. Sorry Annette but the Beach Party is over. I really want to go back to Sydney. He suggests it's to do with me being drunk and nostalgic. He says what I want is an impossibility and calls it our tribe's very own beach story, Beach Story #5, "I wanna go home." I don't understand what he's getting at and fall asleep trying to work it out.

When I wake, it's still night and there's a fierce storm out at sea. He's already awake, sitting on the verandah watching the banks of clouds majestically roll towards our island.

There's a huge surf running and the air is filled with sea spray. We wait, at first entranced by the cosmic flash photography, then, as it gets nearer, we join the crowd gathering in the middle of the nearby thatched roof restaurant.

Everyone is talking too loudly. The fear is instant, almost overwhelming, then recognised and denied. Someone died here last year after being struck by lightening. We should put all our metal jewellery in the middle of the table. There isn't a Western doctor on this island. An American says we needn't worry, he has a Basic Emergency Aid Proficiency Certificate.

"Same same the Challenger astronauts," whispers the English queen.

There's a scramble to get under the biggest table.

The storm hits. The wind and rain are deafeningly loud. The lights go out. The roof comes off a nearby hut and tumbles off into the dark. Each time lightning strikes nearby we can see branches, pieces of galvanised iron and, once, even a plastic chair and table flying past. The universe shakes and splits with delight.

For one terrible, exhilarating minute we are alive at the eye of the storm. The air is electric, my skin's tingling and despite the noise, I can hear my own pulse. Edward grabs my arm. The next flash I can see him clearly, crouched next to me under the table, his face lit up with excitement and wonder.

"Look," he shouts, "On the beach."

I peer out. Another flash of lightning and I can see a solitary figure in a black dress striding along the shore, arms gesturing wildly, wig in one hand, shoes in the other. Next flash, she's gone.

We wait for the storm to pass. And it does, with the same venom and as quickly as it blew in. There's a strong cool breeze followed by gentle rain. We return to our hut and sit on the verandah, taking turns to swig on a bottle of Mekhong.

"Diana's probably halfway to Kansas by now. You didn't see a little dog following her, did you?"

"Half her luck. She just has to get her shoe fixed, click her heels together three times and she'll be back home."

"For me right now," he says, "this is home. You're here and it's a memory we'll always have in common. That's what makes somewhere home. The people you share your life with. A lot of the men I knew in London aren't there any more. That's why it's impossible to go back. If I return, it'll be to start something new. Sure, I'll tell people about the night I bravely faced death in a monsoon storm. About being stuck under a wobbly table with a terrified Supremes revival reject. And about Diana... But it won't be the same as talking about it with you."

This time he makes sense.

In the morning there's debris everywhere. It's a clear, tranquil day. Huts are being repaired. The local fishermen have returned unharmed and the waves are back to plopping gently on the shore. The nearby restaurant is open, business as usual.

Diana, in baggy shorts and an oversized t-shirt, has a huge carry-all slung over one shoulder. She calls to us as she resolutely makes her way along the beach towards the track that leads up to the main road.

"What a dump. Pattaya much better. Bye bye."

We wave back, wishing her luck and promising we'll keep practising for our stage debut.

"Another beach story?" I suggest.

"Toto, I don't think we're in Thailand anymore."

"No-one would believe it."

"What about you? Are you going back to Oz?"

"Not yet," I reply. "But soon."

We order more coffee and settle back to wait for Blue Speedos to emerge and perform his morning ritual of stretching exercises followed by a quick dip.

Gary Dunne

print books
If Blood Should Stain the Lino (inVersions, 1983)
Edge City on Two Different Plans, co-editor, (SGWC, 1983)
As If Overnight (BlackWattle, 1990)
Travelling on Love in a Time of Uncertainty, editor (BlackWattle, 1991)
Shadows on the Dance Floor (BlackWattle, 1992)
Fruit, editor, (BlackWattle, 1994)
Ken Always Does as He's Told (Cheap Red Dress, 2019)
The Other Side of Nowhere (Cheap Red Dress, 2020)
The Darlinghurst Boys (Cheap Red Dress, 2020)

ebooks
Gary was (co-)editor of the many anthologies of contemporary gay fiction the website gay-ebooks.com.au published over the decade or so that that the site was on-line. The site also published his novellas and other work.

cheap red dress is releasing hard copies of his more interesting earlier publications, as well as new, previously unpublished works.

bio
Gary's short fiction has been appearing in anthologies and magazines in Australia and overseas for over 40 years. For decades, he was a regular columnist and arts journalist for various Oz LGBTQI newspapers, magazines and websites. These days he's much more self-indulgent than he used to be.